How to Draw
Fashion Dresses

(Book with Names)

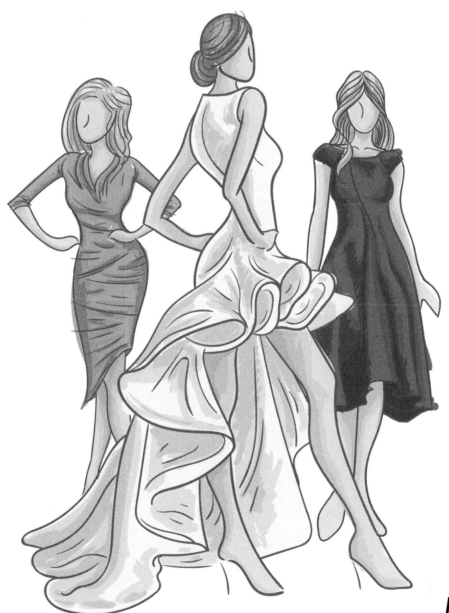

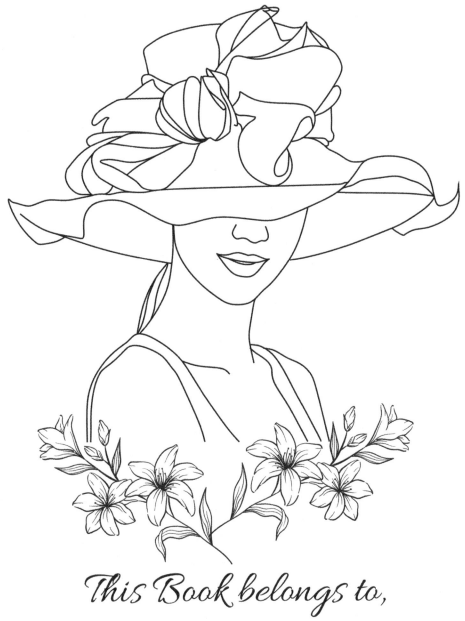

This Book belongs to,

_____

Culotte Dress

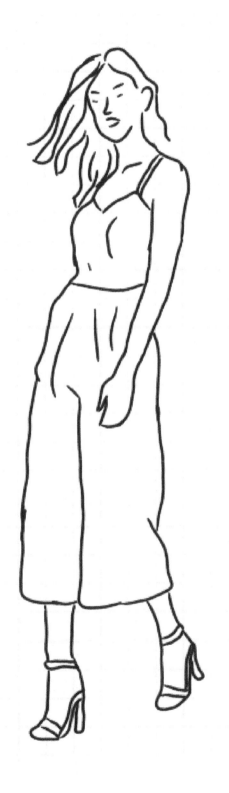

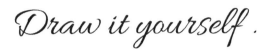

Draw it yourself .

Baby Doll Dress

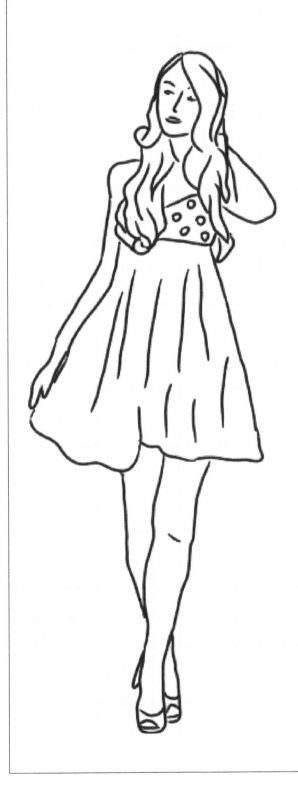

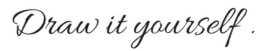

Draw it yourself.

Wrap around Dress

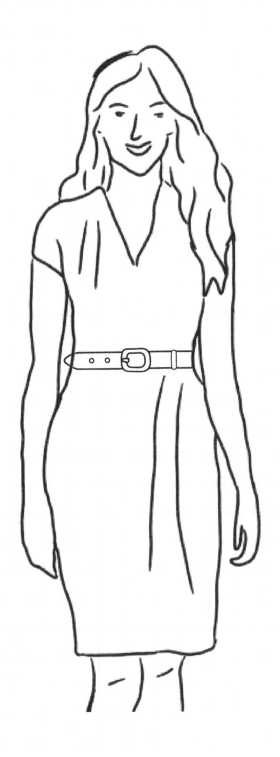

Draw it yourself .

Kimono Dress

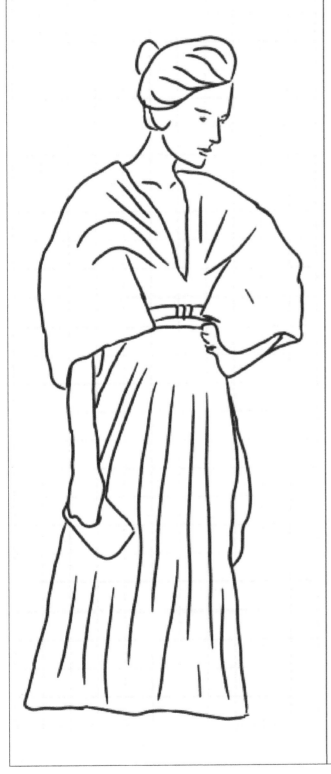

Draw it yourself.

Bubble Dress

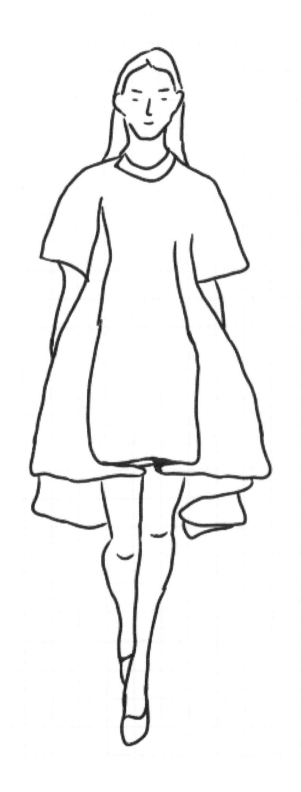

Draw it yourself.

Tutu Dress

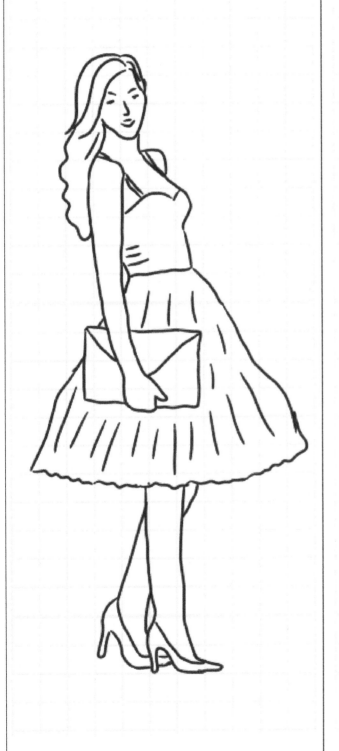

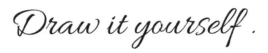

Draw it yourself .

Polo Dress

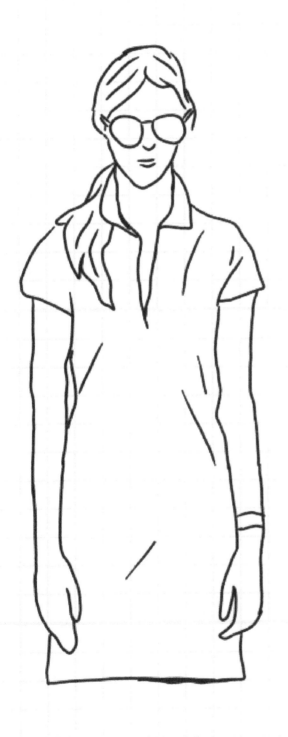

Draw it yourself .

Shirt Dress

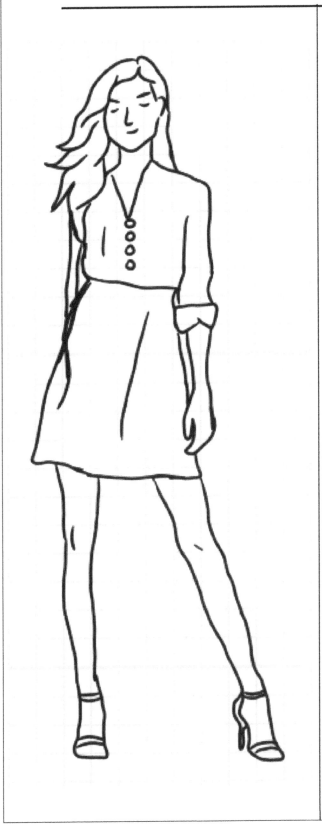

Draw it yourself .

Sun Dress

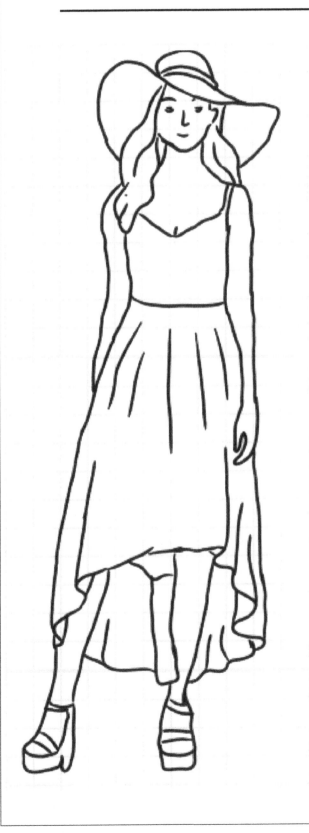

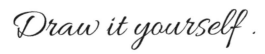

Sari

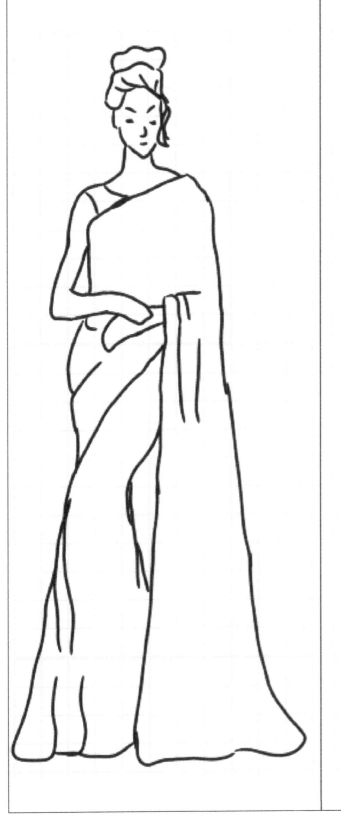

Draw it yourself .

Sack Dress

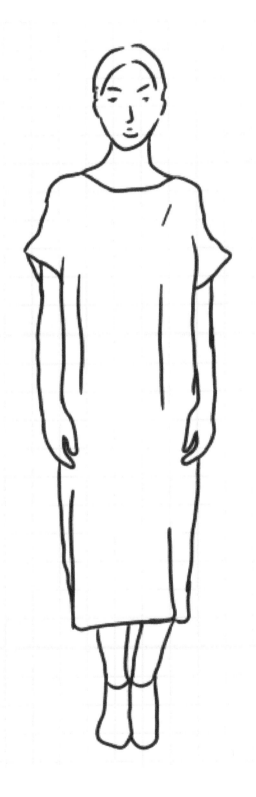

Draw it yourself .

Tunic Dress

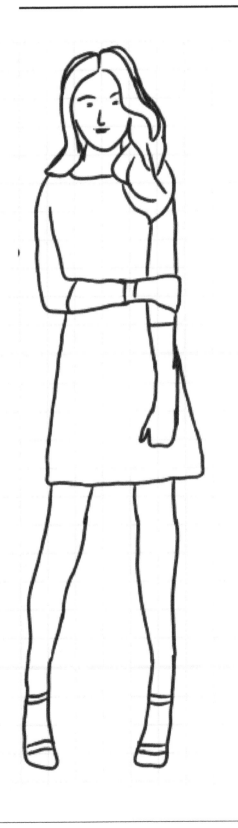

Draw it yourself .

Sheath Dress

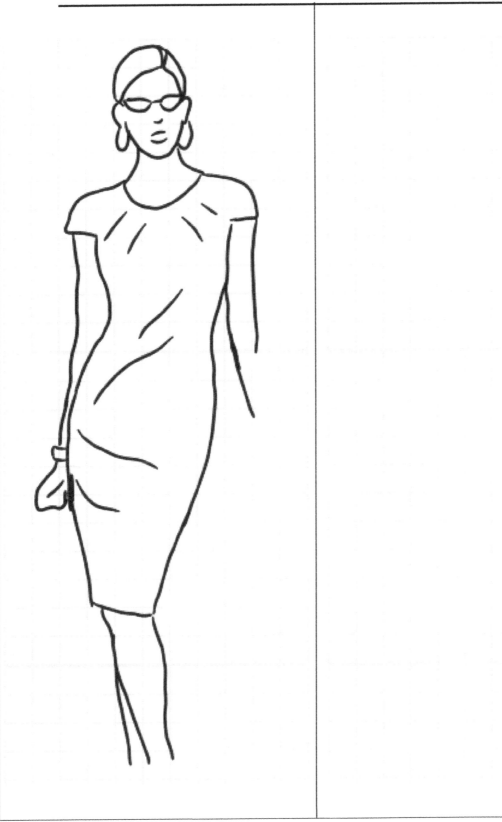

Draw it yourself.

Shift Dress

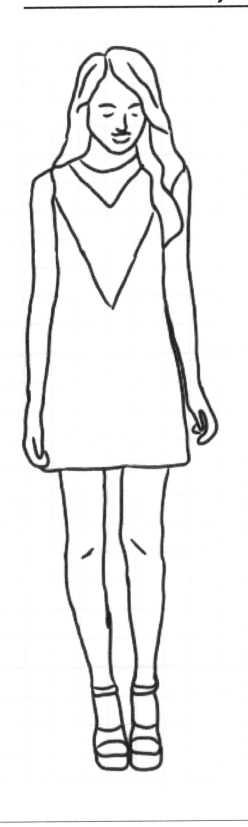

Draw it yourself.

Trumpet Dress

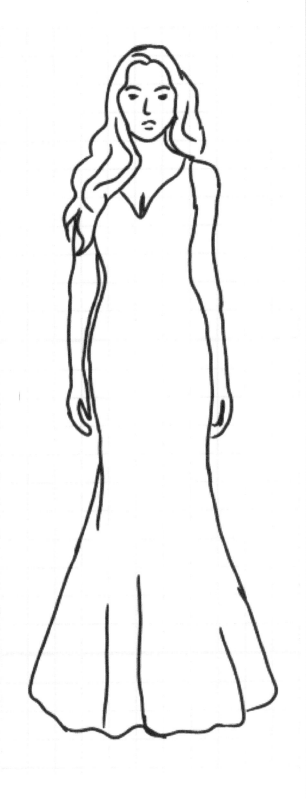

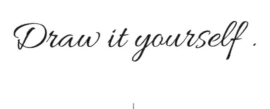

Draw it yourself .

Smoked Dress

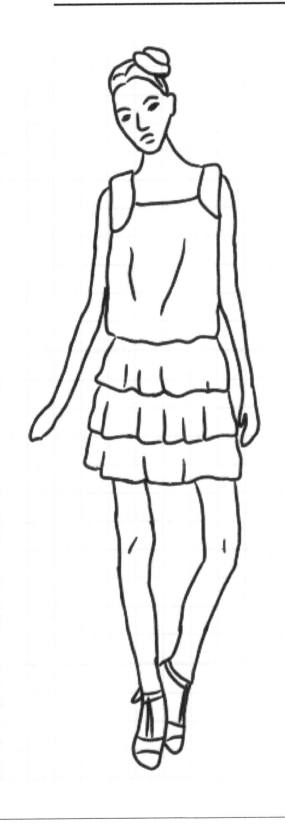

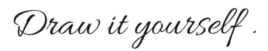

Draw it yourself .

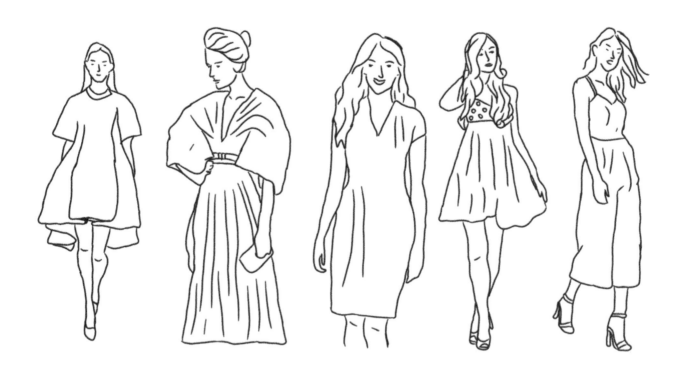

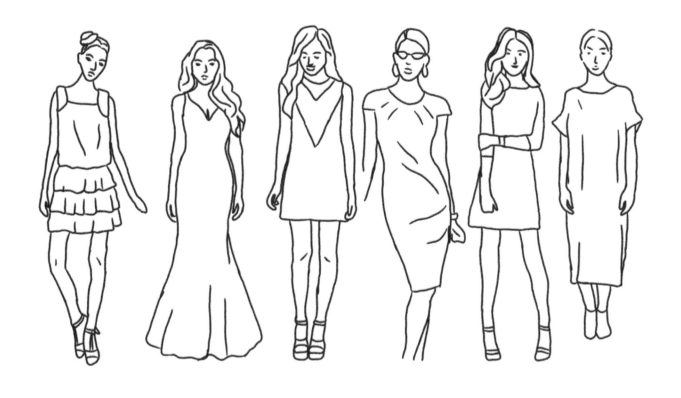

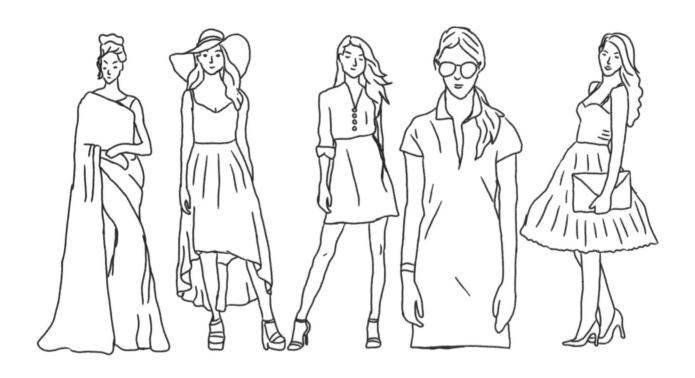

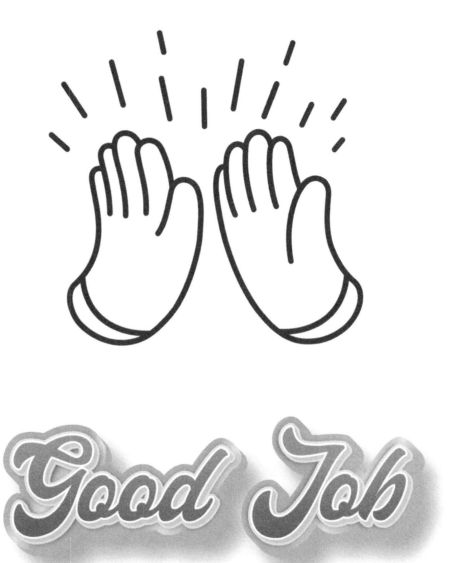

Made in the USA
Monee, IL
20 June 2023

36454293R00044